THE Art OF
A FRESH START!

A Woman's Guide to Healing from the Inside Out!

GWEN CUNNINGHAM

TABLE OF CONTENT

DEDICATION

This book is dedicated to four special women in my life, who have reared, taught, shaped, molded, believed and never gave up on me.

Mother ~ Florence Jones

Grandmother ~ Dorothy Payne

Grandmother ~ Adell Jones

Aunt ~ Mary Guthrie

In addition, my heartfelt gratitude and appreciation to my host of family and friends who love me unconditionally.

ABOUT THE BOOK

The Art of A Fresh Start is today's woman practical guide for inner healing, restoration, inspiration, and empowerment. Whether you've been delayed, abused, denied, divorced, or discounted altogether, this book is dually designed for in-depth conversation or quiet, meditative reflection. Certified Life Coach, Image Consultant and Author, Gwen Cunningham, is solely committed to the development of the "total woman" to heal, to shine and to soar from the inside and out.

You deserve a FRESH start. You deserve to achieve your highest aspirations and dream potential. Discover the art of how to get back UP, get unstuck and get your life moving in the right direction!

www.FreshStartYourLife.com
Facebook: FreshStartwithCoachGwen
Twitter: FreshStartForU
Email: Coach@FreshStartYourLife.com

PREFACE

For years, I felt alone and had no one to identify with. After discovering and connecting with a women's support group, I was able to begin my healing process from the inside out. My journey began with a coach who guided me with a roadmap to blaze a new beginning, which I affectionately refer to as, "My Fresh Start."

As you embrace and absorb the pages in this book, I want you to realize that you are not alone. May you discover the art of healing, wholeness, restoration, wellness, happiness, freedom and unmerited blessing that you so richly are worthy of. Let the pages speak to you and paint a new, bigger, brighter YOU—from the inside out!

~Coach Gwen

THE ART
PART I

FRESH START YOUR *THINKING*

START WITH AWARENESS

This step was the hardest to take, at first. I used to blame my negativity on all kinds of outside forces—fate, experiences, parents, relationships—but I never really stopped to acknowledge, "I'm not the victim." Teaching myself that positivity is a choice has been one of the greatest things I've ever done. Now, when I find myself in a bad situation, I know that it's up to me to find the good; to be positive regardless of what's happening around me. I no longer point fingers and place blame. I realize that everything happens, how it happens, and it's up to me to choose how I want to feel about it. I am in control of my attitude and no one can take that away from me.

START MOVING FORWARD

You are responsible for the complete management of your own thinking.

START TO WIN

❖ *Rid Your Life of Negativity.* If you want to live a positive, joyful life, you cannot be surrounded by negative people who don't encourage your happiness. When I decided to make the change to live a more positive life, I had to rid my life of negative influences. No one is perfect—and perfection isn't the goal when it comes to positivity—but there were people in my life who were consistently negative, who constantly brought me down.

❖ *Look For The Positives.* There is something good in every person and in every situation. Sometimes, you may have to look hard to find the good. When I'm faced with a difficult or challenging situation, I think to myself, "What's good about this?" No matter how terrible the situation might seem, I always can find something good if I take the time to think about it.

❖ *Reinforce Positivity in Yourself.* Once I started thinking more positively, I realized I had to reinforce these thoughts and behaviors in myself in order to make them stick. As with any training, the more you practice, the better you become and yes, you can practice being positive. Be honest with yourself and do your best to look for the good. Whatever you do, refuse to focus on the negative. It's okay not to like everything about yourself, but don't focus on what you don't like. We all have positive attributes, and it's up to you to remind yourself of them every day.

❖ *Share Positivity with Others.* Not only do you need to be positive with yourself in order for this training to really take effect, but you need to be positive with others. You have to share your wealth of positivity with the world. The best way I've found to do this is quite simple and basic: Be nice to other people, no matter what. Tell someone they look nice today. Tell someone they did a great job on that presentation. Believe in yourself and remember the most important lesson of all: A positive outlook is always your choice to make.

START "WRITE" NOW

Journal your thoughts, insights, action items and aha moments at the end of this section!

FRESH START YOUR *ATTITUDE*

START WITH AWARENESS

The main cause of a prevailing negative attitude is generally linked to wrong beliefs about life, at least certain aspects of it. You perceive life through the lens of your beliefs and if your beliefs are negative, your attitude will reflect those beliefs. Change starts with changing your beliefs. I remember complaining about how unhappy I was. It was clear that my unhappiness was linked directly to my negative attitude. It was hard to understand and accept at first, but the sooner I did, the sooner I was able to change for the better. Complaining, alone, kept me stuck in the circumstances that were both miserable and unsatisfying.

START MOVING FORWARD

Confront the reality that certain aspects of your attitude have negative effects and could be holding you back.

START TO WIN

❖ *Always Focus on What You Want Rather Than What You Don't Want.* The mistake that most of us make when having a problem is talking about it over and over again instead of focusing on the end result and what we want to achieve.

❖ *Know That Every Problem Comes With A Lesson.* There is a lesson in everything that happens to us. We should constantly look for what that lesson is and master it. "If you make a mistake and do not correct it, this is called a mistake." ~Confucius

❖ *Don't Believe Everything You Think.* Our problems aren't as big as the mind tries to convince us that they are. If you choose to believe every negative thought that goes through your mind, you'll always get in trouble. Observe your mind, observe your thoughts, but don't identify yourself with them. Go beyond them when necessary.

❖ *Choose to Express Gratitude in Everything.* The more you choose to express your gratitude, whether good or bad, the more reasons you'll have to master the art of a good attitude. When you're busy focusing on the many things that you are grateful for, there will be no more room left for stress, worry and negativity.

START "WRITE" NOW

Journal your thoughts, insights, action items and aha moments at the end of this section!

FRESH START YOUR *CONFIDENCE*

START WITH AWARENESS

Self-confidence cannot have residual effects. If you lack or have low confidence levels, you can severely restrict your motivation, aspiration and enjoyment in life. You can lack esteem and respect. You feel low and find it hard to pick yourself up. Your friends may say pick yourself up, but sometimes things aren't as easy as they may suggest. When you lack or have little self-confidence, it will have an effect on your outlook in terms of what you do, how you approach things, and what you are willing to try. Not to mention, what you leave alone for fear of criticism or fear of failure. I remember I used to chronically complain and blame others; I was suffering from a lack of self-confidence. Subliminally, I took the responsibility off me and placed it on those who I was complaining about. I became the victim.

START MOVING FORWARD

Recognize the signs early and commit to do something about it!

START TO WIN

❖ *Write A Letter!* Write a compassionate letter to yourself, a letter from an older, wiser, and more confident you. What would you say to yourself now, and what would a confident future look like?

❖ *Set Clear Goals.* As you build your self-confidence, what are your goals? What would you like to work on? Ask, "If this is going to help me learn about myself; whichever way it goes, will it help me develop my self-confidence because I will know more at the end of it." Self-compassion gives us the courage and strength to build our self-confidence. It also supports, encourages and empowers us to do what's in our best interests.

❖ *List Your Strengths.* This is a simple task that will help you get into a self-positive mindset, which is essential to maintaining confidence. Yes, you have flaws; everyone does, but often, a lack of confidence is the result of a lack of self-esteem.

❖ *Make Three Lists.* One about your strengths, one about your achievements, and one about the things you admire. Get a friend or relative to help you. Keep the lists in a safe place and read through them regularly.

START "WRITE" NOW

Journal your thoughts, insights, action items and aha moments at the end of this section!

FRESH START YOUR *ESTEEM*

START WITH AWARENESS

As far back as I can remember, I was afraid to dream. I discovered early in my life that I was different. I had a speech impediment (stuttering). I went to grammar school in a prominent white area of Passaic, New Jersey and by the time I entered middle school, I was ridiculed as an Uncle Tom or talking like a white girl. The treatment was cruel. I felt alone, not black, not white— just different. For many years, I was empty inside and never felt good enough to fit in. I built my reality based on my current environment. As discussed earlier, your beliefs determine your attitude and behavior.

START MOVING FORWARD

Understand that your differences should be embraced and celebrated, not buried or hated.

START TO WIN

❖ *Focus **Only** On The Things You Can Change.* Start by doing one thing that builds momentum. Momentum creates the positive energy of accomplishment that fuels action in other areas to IMMEDIATELY move on to doing something else, while your energy is high and thriving.

❖ *Don't Compare Yourself To Others.* Why seek comparisons? If you were the only person in the world, you would not have low self-esteem because there would be no one to compare yourself to. So don't worry what other people are doing or thinking. They think a whole lot LESS about you than you might imagine – they're too wrapped up in their own lives! March to your own drummer, at your own pace, to the best of your ability, and love who you are! Read inspirational stories of regular people doing extraordinary things just to drill it into your head that you CAN do more than you believe you can.

❖ *Use Positive, Helpful Self-Talk.* Avoid affirmations that you feel are untrue i.e. "I am successful and wealthy" if you're barely making rent. It won't work. Instead, focus on action i.e. "I am doing my best, with integrity, with the intention of serving others. I know that abundance is coming my way."

❖ *Do Things You're Good At and What You Love.* What makes you happy? Reinforce your positives, abilities, strengths and talents for a daily dose of self-esteem.

START "WRITE" NOW:

Journal your thoughts, insights, action items and aha moments at the end of this section

FRESH START YOUR *FORGIVENESS*

START WITH AWARENESS

Forgiving yourself can be the most difficult kind of forgiveness to practice. But not forgiving yourself can be destructive. Have you ever noticed how easy it's to hold on to past mistakes long after they occurred? Some of us hold on to things for years! Forgiveness is a process. It does not happen overnight and the process will be different for everyone. But no matter how long it takes, there's a remedy.

START MOVING FORWARD

Get real honest about the hurt you've caused and/or received and embrace the healing process of authentic forgiveness.

START TO WIN

❖ *Clarify Your Core Morals And Values.* The reason most of us feel guilt or shame for actions done in the past is because those actions aren't in line with our current morals and values. Our past wrongs can actually clue us in to what we hold important. By identifying our morals and values, we start to get a clearer picture as to "why" we're hurting over what we've done, or what others did to us.

❖ *Realize That The Past Will Always Remain In The Past.* This seems fairly straightforward, but when we can really accept the fact that we can't undo the past, letting go causes acceptance and increased acceptance can lead to the emotional healing we're all looking for.

❖ *Cut Yourself Some Slack.* When we learned how to ride a bike, most of us realized it would probably take a few tries before achieving perfection. New behavior and thinking patterns are no different;

they're both skills. Cut yourself some slack while you're on a new learning curve. Realize that you're going to make mistakes. We all do.

❖ *Turn The Page.* At some point, you have to accept that the past has happened and you've done everything in your power to amend mistakes. It's now time to turn the page and accept those events as part of your story. They've all contributed to making you who you are. Being grateful for those experiences allows you to move on and truly forgive yourself.

START "WRITE" NOW:

Journal your thoughts, insights, action items and aha moments at the end of this section!

FRESH START YOUR *FREEDOM*

START WITH AWARENESS

My mind was once filled with negative talk and self-doubt. Those thoughts were so loud, I could not hear my authentic, true self shine through. On a deeper level, I knew she existed, but I didn't know how to get to a place in which I could connect with her. I believed I had to work at it, change myself, and somehow be good enough so I could free myself. I believed the key to happiness was figuring out how to "fix" everything that was wrong with me. If I fixed myself, then I could enjoy life and be that free woman I always desired. Little did I know, this wasn't the freedom plan to fix me! My outer world wasn't something that needed to be fixed, changed, or controlled in order for me to experience peace. This outer reality was a direct reflection of my thoughts and as they stayed rooted in negativity, so did my world. Instead, I examined where my thoughts made me feel stuck, trapped, or hopeless.

START MOVING FORWARD

Freedom often begins with what's happening or not happening internally, not externally!

START TO WIN

❖ *Don't Take Anything Personally.* When someone says something to you, whether it's an insult, piece of advice, or anything at all, connect back to your awareness. Only you can know what's true or not. By taking another person's opinion of yourself to heart and choosing to believe it, you are doing yourself a huge injustice.

❖ *Don't Be A Victim.* Embrace each and every thing that happens as an opportunity. When something "bad" happens ask, "What's the universe trying to tell me?" Accept situations as signs or opportunities, and remember that there is a purpose and a greater good to each. Look for the lesson rather than getting stuck in victim mode.

❖ *Know That You're a Priority.* You have to be aware of the fact that you're allowed to make yourself a priority. You are just as valuable as other people. When you feel like you need a break, more attention, or more time by yourself – these are valid. You are the only one who can decide to put yourself first (just like everybody else does).

❖ *Make Your Boundaries Clear.* If you don't have any boundaries, other people won't be able to recognize them. So, take a few moments to contemplate what you want your boundaries to be, both physical and mental. Dig deep and maybe even write a little boundary checklist, so that you can refer back to when you feel like your boundaries are being taken advantage of or when they become diluted and less defined.

START "WRITE" NOW:

Journal your thoughts, insights, action items and aha moments at the end of this section!

START "WRITE" NOW

THINKING

_____

_____

_____

_____

_____

ATTITUDE

_____

_____

_____

_____

_____

CONFIDENCE

_____

_____

_____

_____

_____

ESTEEM

_____
_____
_____
_____
_____

FORGIVENESS

_____
_____
_____
_____
_____

FREEDOM

_____
_____
_____
_____
_____

THE ART
PART II

FRESH START YOUR FAMILY

START WITH AWARENESS

Every family is different in its origin and orientation. I grew up with four siblings, two brothers and two sisters. I was always told that you're just like your father. I didn't take that as a compliment since I never knew him and all I ever heard was that he was crazy and had mental health issues. I was teased and bullied at home and at school. Yet I didn't go quietly into the night. I fought for my place in my family. To protect myself, I developed a good punch and grew a sharp tongue. Some of us come with a lot of baggage from dysfunctional families; others have been fortunate to escape such pain and flourish in a normal, productive, and healthy family structure.

START MOVING FORWARD

Your right and proper perception of family can birth a new way of thinking, doing and being.

START TO WIN

❖ *Communicate Frequently.* With our busy schedules, it's difficult to find sufficient time to spend with one another in meaningful conversation. It's extremely important for families to make time to communicate. Talk in the car. Turn off the TV. Turn off the phone. Eat dinner together. Talk to your children at bedtime. Schedule informal or formal family meetings to talk about important issues that affect your family. There are many creative ways to make time to communicate with other family members.

❖ *Communicate Clearly and Directly.* Healthy families communicate their thoughts and feelings in a clear and direct manner. This is especially important when attempting to resolve problems that arise between family members (i.e., spouse, parent-child). Indirect and vague communication will not only fail to resolve problems, but will also contribute to a lack of intimacy and emotional bonding between family members.

❖ *Be an Active Listener.* An essential aspect of effective communication is listening to what others are saying. Being an active listener involves trying your best to understand the point of view of the other person. Whether you are listening to a spouse or a child, it's important to pay close attention to their verbal and non-verbal messages. As an active listener, you must acknowledge and respect the other person's perspective. For example, when listening to a spouse or child, you should nod your head or say, "I understand," which conveys to the other person that you care about what he or she has to say. Another aspect of active listening is seeking clarification if you don't understand the other family member. This can be done by simply asking, "What did you mean when you said..?" or "Did I understand you correctly?"

❖ *Practice To Be Positive.* While it's often necessary to address problems between family members or to deal with negative situations, effective communication is primarily positive. Marital and family researchers have discovered that unhappy family relationships are often the result of negative communication patterns (e.g., criticism, contempt, defensiveness). Couples who are dissatisfied with their relationships typically engage in more negative interactions than positive. It's important for family members to verbally compliment and encourage one another.

START "WRITE" NOW:

Journal your thoughts, insights, action items and aha moments at the end of this section!

FRESH START YOUR LOVE

START WITH AWARENESS

A core decision of your life, the one that will affect every other decision you make, is the commitment to love and accept yourself. It directly affects the quality of your relationships, your work, your free time, your faith, and your future. For many, why is this so difficult to do?

We can only love someone else to the degree to which we love ourselves. This is the prerequisite to receiving life's greatest treasure: LOVE! Self-love is the art of completely accepting our faults, appreciating our gifts, and acknowledging our individuality. *(Individuality is the uniqueness that separates, and sometimes isolates us, from everyone else.)* Once this is achieved, we are ready to love and be loved by another person.

For many years, I was an expert in this area of my life. I was looking for love in all the wrong places. With all my baggage and insecurities, I just wanted to feel love. Not having a father in my life, I was constantly looking for someone to protect me. I'm an incest and rape survivor. For years, I turned to drugs and alcohol to ease my pain. I had no idea what love was or how to love. Finally in 1994, I gave up and wanted to die. After working diligently through my childhood issues, old thoughts, beliefs, and events, I felt alive again. It was like stripping off several layers of paint from an antique piece of furniture. I found myself restored to my original beauty.

START MOVING FORWARD

Your love tank should stay on full, and filled with the right kind of love for giving and receiving.

START TO WIN

❖ *Begin Your Day With Love (Not Technology).* Remind yourself of your worthiness before getting out of bed. Breathe in love and breathe out love. Enfold yourself in light. Saturate your being in love. Take time to meditate and journal. Spend time focusing inward daily. Begin with 5 minutes of meditation and 5 minutes of journaling each morning. Gradually increase this time.

❖ *Get Emotionally Honest.* Let go of numbing your feelings, for example, shopping, eating, and drinking to avoid discomfort, sadness, and pain. Mindfully breathe your way through your feelings and emotions.

❖ *Become Willing To Surrender.* Breathe, relax, and let go. You can never see the whole picture. You don't know what everything is for. Stop fighting against yourself by thinking and desiring people and events in your life should be different.

❖ *Work on Personal and Spiritual Development.* Be willing to surrender and grow. Life is a journey. We're here to learn and love on a deeper level. Take penguin steps and life becomes progressive. One step at a time is enough to proceed forward. Be patient with yourself. Let go of urgency and fear. Relax and transform striving into thriving.

START "WRITE" NOW

Journal your thoughts, insights, action items and aha moments at the end of this section!

FRESH START YOUR FRIENDS

START WITH AWARENESS

Do you have healthy friendships? How is your relationship with your friends? The building of healthy relationships and friendships is an art that many people don't know about. Many people don't know how to deal with others and hence, fail to make close friends and continue to deteriorate existing relationships. Studies show that people who are selfish and greedy don't get to make many close relationships. Since the majority of people don't like to have friends who are selfish or who try to exploit others to get what they want. Your relationship with people is an art that you have to keep working on, so you can build and maintain healthy friendships among your colleagues, acquaintances, and purposeful connections. I have experienced a lot of unhealthy friendships in my life. You attract who you are. The healthier you become, you magnetize friendships that are solid and healthy.

START MOVING FORWARD

Stop and take a good and honest assessment and evaluation of your current friendships.

START TO WIN

❖ *Keep Your Friendships Rewarding*. Sometimes when you have known people for a long time, you can start to take them for granted. This doesn't have to be the case. Always thank your friend when he or she does something for you. Return favors when your friend goes out of his or her way to help you. Tell your friend how much you appreciate them. This doesn't have to be an awkward or long-winded speech that you have prepared. It can be as simple as, "Hey, thanks for always being there for me. I appreciate it."

❖ *Show Interest in Your Friend's Life*. A good friendship should be two-sided — and hopefully, you have a friend who shows interest in you as well. Be a good listener. When your friend talks to you about something that's going on in his or her life, listen. Good relationships are built on communication, so don't ignore your friend. Take the time to really hear what they're saying, and offer advice only if they ask for it.

❖ *Support Each Other When Things Get Rough.* Sometimes friendships can get rocky or friends can have a hard time dealing with their own personal problems. Though it may not be fun, these are situations where a real friend has to step in and be there. Demonstrate your support. Tell your friend, "I'm here for you. Just let me know what you need and I'll help you out." Offer to listen. If there are personal or family problems going on, tell your friend that you are always there when they need to vent. Provide encouragement. If your friend is going through a breakup, come over and spend time with them so they don't feel alone. Take them out to do things to get their mind off the problem. You can go out to eat, a movie, or even a walk.

❖ *Make Sure To Maintain Contact.* If one friend moves far away, keep in touch. People often move far away to go to different schools or pursue a new career. That doesn't mean the friendship has to end. Call your friend regularly. If you don't see each other often, it's important to check in so that you know what's going on in your friend's life. Visit whenever you can. When you are in town, make the time to see your friend. Plan a day of fun sightseeing together, or ask them to show you their favorite things to do.

START "WRITE" NOW

Journal your thoughts, insights, action items and aha moments at the end of this section!

FRESH START YOUR FAITH

START WITH AWARENESS

Most of us are pretty good at worrying unnecessarily. We ask ourselves, *"What if I lose my job?"*, *"What if it rains and ruins the party?"*, *"What if I suddenly get sick?"* What if, what if, what if... Do we give ourselves the chance to ask the positive "What If..." questions such as "What if there is more to life than this?" What if there really is a God? There was a time in my life when I had a 911 relationship with God. The truth is I trusted my own power and played God in all areas of my life. I was raised in church; however all I heard about was a punishing and vengeful God who was waiting to punish me for my sins. So for years I only trusted me. Not until I went through some dark times in my life and wanted to give up on life I had to find a power greater than me if I was going to live. Having strong faith became an important element in my life. Faith is the one thing that can get you through just about any situation no matter how tough it may seem or feel. By having strong faith, you'll feel more confident and at ease because you'll know who to turn to - God.

START MOVING FORWARD

Faith affects all aspects of your life and will make you a better person overall.

START TO WIN

* *Study The Bible*. Receive the word of God. Faith comes by hearing and then applying the word of God. Let us pray! We shouldn't try to impress God with selfish, distant prayers. We need to be honest with God about whatever we're facing at that moment.

* *Love Your (Fellow) Brethren*. Most agree that they love God whom they have not seen - so we should have no problem loving our sisters and brothers that we see every day. God reveals himself to us through His Son, The Holy Spirit, His Love and His people.

❖ *Make A Habit To Meditate*. Think on the word of God. Meditating on the word reveals how to act. Your confessions and testimonials of the word and things of God is part of prayer and meditation. When you read, digest and speak the word to yourself.

❖ *Learn To Forgive*. Don't hold grudges or hold onto things that are out of your control. Let go of the past and forgive those that have caused you pain. Not only will you be more stressed out but you'll carry an unnecessary burden upon your shoulders. Turn to God for guidance and let go of the past.

START "WRITE" NOW

Journal your thoughts, insights, action items and aha moments at the end of this section!

FRESH START YOUR SPIRITUALITY

START WITH AWARENESS:

"Spirituality is awareness that there is something far greater than we are, something that created this universe, created life and that we are an authentic, important, significant part of it, and can contribute to its evolution. At the core of spirituality is the need to feel and express love and compassion for everyone, with the understanding that we are all part of a greater reality." - Elisabeth Kubler-Ross

According to sources, *"Spirituality is the wellspring of divinity that pulsates, dances, and flows as the source and essence of every soul. Spirituality relates more to your personal search, to finding greater meaning and purpose in your existence."* I remember when I had low self-esteem and didn't feel a part of anything. My thinking and outlook on life was very shallow. Today, I love the woman I have become. I have true meaning and purpose.

START MOVING FORWARD

Keep in perspective; you are a part of a greater whole to make the world stronger, richer and better.

START TO WIN

* *Be a River, Not a Swamp.* The Bible says: "Rivers of living water will flow from the heart of those who believe in me" (John 7:38, margin).* Remember, it's the mountain stream that carries fresh, life-giving water because it flows out. However, the swamp is stagnant and life-devouring. A swamp collects and retains water that comes its way. Don't be the kind of person who seeks to accumulate much before allowing a little to flow through.

* *Identify Your Blessings.* Too often we go through life oblivious to the good that comes flowing into our lives. Try this spiritual exercise for one week: At the end of the first day, identify a blessing that came to you from a family member. At the end of the second day, a blessing from a neighbor. Third day, from a friend. Fourth day, from a work colleague. Fifth day,

from a stranger. Sixth day, from a child. On the seventh day, a blessing that came from an "enemy."

❖ *Take A Step Of Faith*. Spiritual growth means taking a leap of faith from time to time. Rather than trying to get everything in place before you start something important, why not follow God's leading and allow the plan to evolve? This means taking a step of faith and trusting God to provide what may be needed for success.

❖ *Have An Attitude of Gratitude*. Start every day with a morning prayer of gratitude to God for the gift of a new day. Do this even if the day ahead appears ominous. Conclude every day with an evening prayer of gratitude to God for the gift of the preceding hours. Do this even if you've had a very tough day.

START "WRITE" NOW

Journal your thoughts, insights, action items and aha moments at the end of this section!

FRESH START YOUR PURPOSE

START WITH AWARENESS

"What's my purpose in life?" - is a question asked by many as they ponder the reasons for their existence. Life is the expression of the Reason for being. The Reason represents the intelligence that is within all things. For example, it's the power within a seed, when planted in the garden, grows step by step to the fulfilment of its reason for being. Autumn is a wonderful example of the fulfilment of many plants as we enjoy the abundance of fruits and vegetables that are harvested at this time in the cycles or seasons of life. The real you is your inner purpose. When you took your first breath of life, you became a purposeful being. The time of birth determines the quality of the power within you and reveals your purpose in life.

START MOVING FORWARD

Everything has a purpose, a time and a season.

START TO WIN

❖ *Discover Your Talents and Gifts.* What's your unique ability, the skill or skills which, if truly actualize, could provide significant benefits to your family, business, career, community and world at large?

❖ *Pinpoint Your Passions.* What do you love to do, that you would do, even if you don't get paid for it? What is it that you just have to do, no matter what?

❖ *Major In What Matters Most.* What's the one thing you want to experience, or do, or accomplish, before you die, so that on your last day on earth you feel satisfied and have no regrets?

❖ *Pay Attention to Confirmations.* What do other people say you're really good at? People often tell me that they feel better, uplifted and energized, after spending time talking with me. Not too surprising then, that I now spend my life and even earn my living encouraging others and helping them improve their lives.

START "WRITE" NOW

Journal your thoughts, insights, action items and aha moments at the end of this section!

START "WRITE" NOW

FAMILY

_____

_____

_____

_____

_____

LOVE

_____

_____

_____

_____

_____

FRIENDS

_____

_____

_____

_____

FAITH

_____

_____

_____

_____

_____

SPIRITUALITY

_____

_____

_____

_____

_____

PURPOSE

_____

_____

_____

_____

_____

THE ART

PART III

FRESH START YOUR BEAUTY

START WITH AWARENESS

"The beauty of a woman is not in actual appearance, but true beauty in a Woman is reflected in her soul. It is the caring that she lovingly gives, the passion that she knows. The wise don't buy into other people's perceptions of who they are and what they are capable of. Instead, they bypass a person's public persona and see who they are in their highest expression. When you see actions taken with integrity, instead of words only, you will then know a soul's worth." –Audrey Hepburn

Beauty can be something that's based on physical features for many people, but TRUE beauty is something that's within and without—or inside out! It's when you're smiling outside and has a radiant personality to match. It's when you light up a whole room without even trying. When you take care of yourself physically, treat everyone equally and make sure you never make anyone feel like they aren't good enough. True beauty isn't the "pretty" girl that wears pounds and pounds of makeup and a fake tan to look fabulous. True beauty comes from the girl that wears no makeup and doesn't even have to tan to look beautiful, and yet she does. That's what true beauty is, and not everyone can see that.

START MOVING FORWARD

Embrace that real beauty is never tangible, but intangible.

START TO WIN

❖ *Mirror Affirmations*. Try to look in the mirror every day and think to yourself, "I am beautiful whether other people agree or disagree." Love yourself no matter what the odds are. Be thankful for who you are and what you see yourself as because we all know that there are others who have it far worse than we do.

❖ *Stay Confident*. It's easier said than done but if you see yourself as healthy, strong, and independent then other people will start to see it as well. Make time for yourself. Most of us have families, jobs, businesses or are in school, and we forget to make time for ourselves.

❖ *Set Goals for Yourself*. Practice achieving your goals every day, whether it's self-confidence or building up a healthier life style.

❖ *Take Pride In Yourself*. But remember this. No one is perfect and there is no such thing as perfection in this world. Don't strive to shape your image to what you see in the magazines. Don't try to impersonate/mimic the life style of a model. This is NOT what I'm trying to achieve, and you shouldn't either.

START "WRITE" NOW

Journal your thoughts, insights, action items and aha moments at the end of this section!

FRESH START YOUR (INNER) IMAGE

START WITH AWARENESS

Your personal image is how you are perceived by others. Many different things go into your image such as non-verbal communication. Although the spoken word does carry weight as we develop rapport. Initially we're judged by what people see. Each time you meet someone new, they will evaluate you either consciously or subconsciously. They will notice your clothing, your hairstyle, and your accessories. They will notice how you are groomed and how you carry yourself. Every aspect of how you appear is pieced together forming a picture or an interpretation of your image. This interpretation will lead to their comfort level about you and help them determine whether they will listen to you.

It's surprising how often, and how natural, it is to judge oneself. Have you ever asked yourself "what was I thinking" or thought "that was stupid." after doing something? That was your internal voice judging you. For some, that internal voice can be too critical and harsh, leading to low self-esteem. For others, it may be so weak that they don't notice when they are mean or insensitive to others. Listening to your internal voice and judgments is the first step to changing your self-image and esteem. One way to gain a better understanding of your current self-image is to imagine your reaction to certain situations. For example, if you start a beautiful morning thinking, "I can't wait to get outside and do things!" you are exhibiting a more positive internal voice. Instead of chiding yourself for not getting out of bed thinking, "don't be such a lazy slob, start moving!" Sometimes it's hard not to listen to an internal voice, even when that voice is critical. Sometimes a person passes internal judgments to protect him or herself from potentially awkward or uncomfortable situations. For example, telling yourself you aren't able to do something or convincing yourself that others won't like you is a way of avoiding potential failure or rejection. Because of this, people often put up with internal criticisms, even though they lead to low self-esteem. But it's possible to protect yourself without limiting yourself. For example, you could place less importance on other's opinions of you *("so what if* they don't like me?"), or emphasize the positive *("at least I wasn't afraid to try")*. You can also practice silencing or correcting your internal voice when it exaggerates your negative traits. It's important that when you make internal judgments, you also listen to the more rational part of yourself that can adjust for any unreasonable criticism.

START MOVING FORWARD

Be aware of what shapes and reshapes your inner image and only focus on the positives that will adjust, correct, improve or add to it!

START TO WIN

❖ *Nip Negative Thoughts in the Bud*. Sometimes putting a stop on negative thinking is as easy as that. The next time you start giving yourself an internal browbeating, tell yourself to "stop it!" If you saw a person yelling insults at another person for no apparent reason, you would probably tell them to stop. Why do you accept that behavior from yourself?

❖ *Focus on a Different Perspective*. Instead of focusing on what you think are your negative qualities, accentuate your strengths and assets. Maybe you didn't ace the test you were studying for, but your hard work and perseverance led to a better grade than you would have had. Maybe you felt nervous and self-conscious when giving a presentation at work, but your boss and coworkers respected you for getting up and trying.

❖ *Replace Criticism With Encouragement.* Instead of nagging or focusing on the negative (in yourself and others), replace criticism with encouragement. Give constructive criticism instead of being critical *("maybe if I tried to do ____ next time, it would be even better" instead of "I didn't do that right.")* Compliment yourself and those around you on what you have achieved *("well, we may not have done it all, but we did a pretty great job with what we did".)*

❖ *Ponder on What's Possible!* Avoid *"can't"* thinking or other negative language. If you say something often enough, you may start to believe it, so keep your statements positive. Don't be afraid to seek help in accomplishing goals, but remind yourself that you don't need approval from others to recognize your accomplishments. Focus on what you're able to do. Remind yourself of all your capabilities and positive qualities.

START "WRITE" NOW

Journal your thoughts, insights, action items and aha moments at the end of this section!

FRESH START YOUR (OUTER) IMAGE

START WITH AWARENESS

First impressions are important - they can be about attitude as well as dress. Visual impact is at least as important as verbal impact. People will quickly make assumptions based on your facial expressions, the clothes you wear, how well-groomed you are and your body language.

All individuals change their approach depending on the people they meet and what they feel is expected from them. Your *on-duty* self, the one who functions in public, is different from your *off-duty* self, the one at home with family and friends. Everyone has many and varied roles in life. You can be one person and still be a parent, son/daughter, brother/sister, friend, adviser, patient, client and consumer all in one day. These differing roles all require their own particular qualities and skills in personal communication and can also call upon different requirements of attitude and appearance, i.e., of visual image. Your outer image (appearance) is how you are seen by the world.

I remember when I thought it was all about how I looked. I had an arrogant attitude and walked around like the world owed me something. Not until I started working on my inside to match my outside, all I really had were nice clothes to adorn my body.

START MOVING FORWARD

The main key is to marry (make one) your inner image with your outer image.

START TO WIN

- ❖ *Discover What's Broken*. Know what the problem is so that you know what to fix. Is it apparel, teeth, hair, style, grooming, etc.?
- ❖ *Take A Wardrobe And Personal Image Assessment*. You can learn how to improve your dress, but also gain a new personal outlook. Making changes to your personal appearance can make you a more confident person that's more in-tune with your goals.

❖ *Develop a Sharp(er) Image.* In my experience, having a sharp image improves your life significantly. It means you have the self confidence and trust of others and you have their respect—at least from a first impression perspective. It also means looking good on the outside and feeling good on the inside.

❖ *Adopt The Power Image.* It's made up of your voice, your posture, your smile, and the way you dress. It includes aspects of your overall image that culminates the belief that you deserve respect and have the power to accomplish anything.

START "WRITE" NOW

Journal your thoughts, insights, action items and aha moments at the end of this section!

FRESH START YOUR STYLE

START WITH AWARENESS

Style goes way beyond fashion. It's an individually distinctive way of putting ourselves together. It's a unique blend of spirit and substance—personal identity imposed on and created through, the world of things. It's a way of capturing something vibrant, making a statement about ourselves via apparel. It's what people really want when they aspire to be fashionable. Style is one part personality: spirit, attitude, wit, and inventiveness. It demands the desire and confidence to express whatever mood one wishes. Such variability is not only necessary but a reflection of a person's unique complexity as a human being. People want to be themselves and to be seen as themselves. In order to work, style must reflect the real self, the character and personality of the individual; anything less appears to be a costume.

Lastly, style is one part fashion. It's possible to have plenty of clothes and not an ounce of style. But it's also possible to have very few clothes and lots of style. Yes, fashion is the means through which we express style, but it takes less concerning clothes to be stylish than you might imagine. That's why generations of women have coveted the little black dress, a garment so unassuming in line and perfect in proportion that it's the finest foil for excursions into self-expression. I remember when I didn't have any substance; I used clothes as a way to look on the outside. I appeared to have it all together but in reality I was a well-dressed garbage can. When I did the necessary work on my inside (internally), then my style became more radiant, and attitude more positive. I reflected true beauty and style!

START MOVING FORWARD

Discover your true style and make it a lifestyle!

START TO WIN

- ❖ *Know What Matters Most*. This is really important, because you can be very stylish, but feel bad because you hate the clothes that you're wearing. Figure out (or at least get an idea) of the type of clothing that you like, so that you can be stylish and know that the clothes you're wearing help express your personality well.

- ❖ *Ditch The Brand Name Clothes*. The most important rule of having style is not to be defined by labels. You won't have your own individual style if you're defined by them. You don't need to wear Gucci or American Eagle to be a stylish person. You can easily be envied even when sporting apparel from Citi Trends or Target!

- ❖ *Know When Clothes Fit You.* Not all of us can have the size 0 body of a model, and that's okay. You don't need that to have style. To have style, you need to know what clothes fit you best, and what styles flatter your body type.

- ❖ *Know How To Put Outfits Together*. You can have a lot of nice single pieces of clothing, but you're lacking style if you don't know how to put them together. Know what colors work well together, and how to avoid a boring outfit. Know when to rock the heels and when to go for some sneakers. **Be** confident and wear your clothes—don't let your clothes wear *you*!

START "WRITE" NOW

Journal your thoughts, insights, action items and aha moments at the end of this section!

START "WRITE" NOW

BEAUTY

_____
_____
_____
_____
_____

IMAGE (INNER)

_____
_____
_____
_____
_____

IMAGE (OUTER)

_____
_____
_____
_____
_____

STYLE

_____

_____

_____

_____

_____

ABOUT THE AUTHOR

GWEN CUNNINGHAM

Class. Confidence. Charisma. Compassion.

Gwen's journey in life was no walk on easy street. She faced and overcame many adversities including physical and mental setbacks. But the tenacious warrior in her wouldn't allow her to give up or cave in but to make an irrevocable commitment that she'd share her story, learned lessons, and relevant life experiences for the betterment and transformation of others.

With an upbeat, energetic, and striking persona that inspires women to approach everyday life with expectancy and positivity, she creates a safe place and space for mutual trust, respect and meaningful dialogue to offer solutions and strategies to win!

Coach Gwen's passion has propelled her to bring out the BEST in everyone she's privileged to work with as a Certified Life Coach and Image Consultant, via personal and professional life coaching, image consulting, mentoring and speaking.

Fresh Start Coaching Programs with Gwen Cunningham

"Coaching, for me, is something I've always done throughout my life, in one form or another with just about everyone I meet. I believe in the total package from the inside out. "

As a Certified Life Coach and Image Consultant, Gwen is enthusiastic to share tips, tools and strategies to overcome obstacles and gain a fresh start at living their best lives in every area.

How much opportunity has passed you by because you lacked the confidence to go after it? And have you ever walked in a room and had that unsettled feeling that you could look better? Furthermore, you may have unknowingly lost engagements because your competition looked more dynamic and professional than you. Like it or not, others DO judge a book by its cover therefore we cannot sell ourselves short and sabotage our success by looking ordinary instead of extraordinary.

Secondly, the "inside" is MORE important that the outside. So, when you join a coaching program with Coach Gwen, you will also gain the proper path to purpose, self-worth, self-identification, personal empowerment and that's just the tip of the iceberg! Are you ready for your FRESH start?

*Watch Me Win: 1-on-1 Coaching Program

*Winner's Circle: Group Coaching Program

*From the Inside Out V.I.P. Coaching Program

Contact Coach Gwen to discuss the right type of services for you. www.freshstartyourlife.com

www.ingramcontent.com/pod-product-compliance
Lightning Source LLC
Chambersburg PA
CBHW072208090426
42740CB00012B/2437